These Are My Senses

What Can I Taste?

Joanna Issa

Heinemann LIBRARY

Chicago, Illinois

© 2015 Heinemann Library
an imprint of Capstone Global Library, LLC
Chicago, Illinois

Edited by Siân Smith
Designed by Richard Parker and Peggie Carley
Picture research by Tracy Cummins
Production by Victoria Fitzgerald
Originated by Capstone Global Library Ltd
Printed in the United States of America in
Eau Claire, Wisconsin. 032818 000332

Library of Congress Cataloging-in-Publication Data
Cataloging-in-publication information is on file with the Library of Congress.
ISBN 978-1-4846-0430-4 (paperback)
ISBN 978-1-4846-0443-4 (eBook PDF)

Photo Credits

Corbis: © Ocean, 15, © Sam Diephuis, front cover; Dreamstime: © Artranq, 10; Getty Images: Cultura/Lisbeth Hjort, 8; iStock: © Rdvan Çelik, 13; Shutterstock: © Eduard Stelmakh, 5, © EMprize, 6, 20 left, 22 left, back cover, © Gelpi JM, 7, © isarescheewin, 4, 21 right, © jerrysa, 12, © Johan Larson, 9, 22 right, © Karen H. Ilagan, 17, © Kesu, 14, 21 left, © Lana Langlois, 18, 20 right, © Olga Miltsova, 16, © Vitaly Korovin, 11, © Zurijeta, 19

Contents

What Can I Taste?

I taste a strawberry.

It is sweet.

I taste a lemon.

It is **sour**.

I taste popcorn.

It is **salty**.

I taste a chili pepper.

It is spicy.

I taste cotton candy.

It is sweet.

I taste limes.

They are sour.

I taste olives.

They are salty.

I taste chocolate.

It is sweet.

Quiz: Spot the Difference

Which foods are sour?

21 The lemons and limes are sour foods.
The strawberry and chocolate are sweet.

Picture Glossary

 **salty**

 **sour**

Index

22

Notes For Teachers and Parents

BEFORE READING

Building background:

Ask children to name a favorite food. Why do they like it? Has it always been their favorite food? Why do they think different people like to eat different things?

AFTER READING

Recall and reflection:

Which foods taste salty? (popcorn, olives) Which foods taste sour? (lemons, limes) Which foods taste sweet? (strawberries, cotton candy, chocolate) Do children prefer foods that taste salty or sweet?

Sentence knowledge:

Ask children to look at page 5. How many sentences are on this page? What type of punctuation mark is used at the end of the sentence?

Word knowledge (phonics):

Encourage children to point at the word *taste* on page 4. Sound out the four phonemes in the word $t/\bar{a}/s/t$. Ask children to sound out each phoneme as they point at the letters and then blend the sounds together to make the word *taste*. Challenge them to say some words that rhyme with the word *taste*. (paste, waste)

Word recognition:

Have children find the word *sweet* on page 5. How many more times can they find it in the book?

EXTENDING IDEAS

Make four columns on a piece of paper. At the top of each column, write one of these headings: sweet, sour, salty, spicy. Give children food magazines or store advertisements to look through to find examples of different foods. Have children cut out pictures and paste them in the correct spots on the chart. Then ask children to decide which is their favorite taste.

In This Book

Topic

tastes and senses

Sentence stems

1. I taste _____.
2. It is _____.
3. They are _____.

High-frequency words

a

are

I

is

it

they